Lila and Andy learn about

The Journey of Electricity!

From Power Plant to Plug

Revised & Updated Second Edition

Kenneth Adams

Book Cover by Kenneth Adams
Illustrations and Images by Kenneth Adams
Illustrations and Images created with AI Assistance
Second Edition 2025

ISBN: 978-1-998552-31-3

Electricity powers our world, but always treat it with respect.
It's as dangerous as it is essential.

This book belongs to:

_____

Hey there! I'm Lila, and I have a question for you. Do you love the great outdoors as much as I do? Camping under the stars, hiking up the snowy slopes of a mountain, or paddleboarding on a crystal-clear lake, these are the things that fill my heart with joy.

My brother Andy is my adventure buddy. Our days are always exciting, filled with new experiences. Together, Andy and I consider every day an opportunity for new and exciting discoveries!

Hi! I'm Andy. One of my many passions is music. I don't really have a favorite style. I just enjoy listening to anything from rock to the catchy beats of pop music.

When I'm not strumming the ukulele, I'm teaching myself to play the guitar, and I've recently started experimenting with a digital keyboard. I'm always finding new tunes to play and create.

Lila is my awesome sister. Whether we're going on road trips with Mom and Dad, or making up our own adventure, we always have the best time!

Electricity has become a very important part of our lives. Almost everything we do, whether we're watching television or playing games on the computer, when we're at school or shopping at the mall, everything needs electricity to work.

We've become so used to always having electricity available to us that it's only when the power goes out that we realize how little we can do without it.

But have you ever wondered where it comes from, and how it gets to your house? Well, take a seat, because today we'll share with you the journey electricity takes to get from where it is made, all the way to your house.

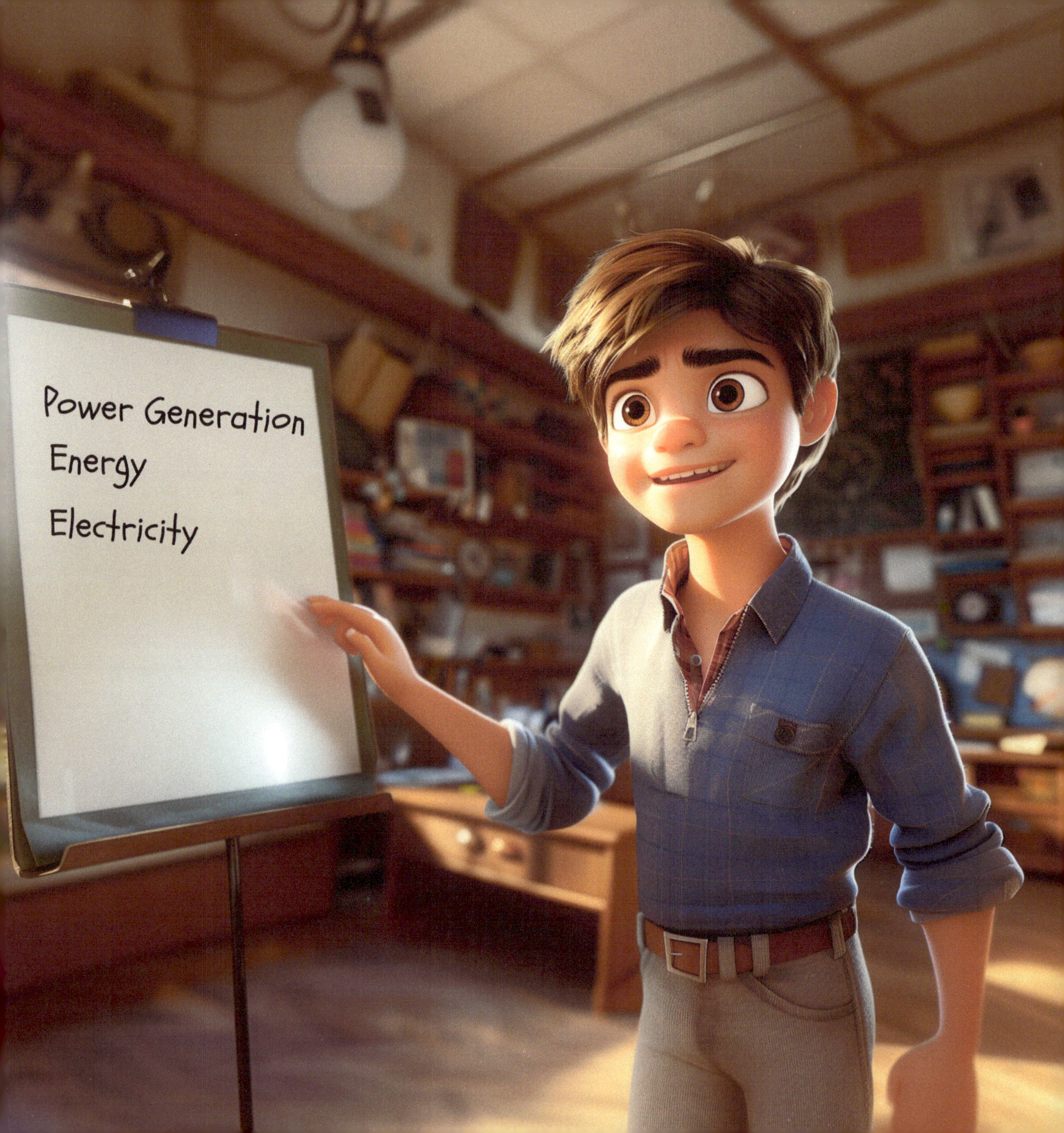
Power Generation
Energy
Electricity

Before we jump into the details of how electricity is made, let's first look at some new words that will make it much easier to understand.

Power: In this book, when we use the word "power", we're talking about electric power or electricity.

Power Generation: To generate something means to create or to make something. Power generation means to make or create power or electricity.

Energy: Energy is the ability to do work. Energy makes things move and grow. When we are tired, we don't have much energy, and it's more difficult to do things, but when we are well-rested and have loads of energy, it's much easier to run around and play. Like we need energy to do things, so do the machines we use to make electricity.

Turbine: A turbine is a type of engine that uses the force of a moving fluid, such as water or steam, to spin blades. As the blades rotate, they generate rotational energy that can be changed into electricity by using a generator.

Generator: A generator is a machine that changes the rotational energy created by turbines into electric energy or electricity. Generators work by using magnets and coils of wire that move near each other. When the magnets spin around the wire coils, they create electricity, similar to how rubbing a balloon on your hair creates static electricity.

Turbine

Generator

Now that we know what these new words mean, let's talk about Power Plants.

Power plants are the factories that create electricity. Since electricity can be made in a couple of different ways, there are different types of power plants.

Let's explore some of the most common ones used to generate power.

Fossil Fuel Power Plants

Power plants that use fuel like coal or natural gas to generate electricity are called fossil fuel power plants. The reason for this is that the fuel they use, coal and natural gas, is formed from the remains of ancient plants and tiny sea creatures that became fossils over millions of years.

A fossil is the preserved remains of plants and animals whose dead bodies were buried in sand and mud, and over millions of years, were turned into rock. The most common types of fossil fuel power plants are coal-fired power plants and natural gas power plants.

Hundreds of millions of years ago, ancient forests and swamps covered the Earth.

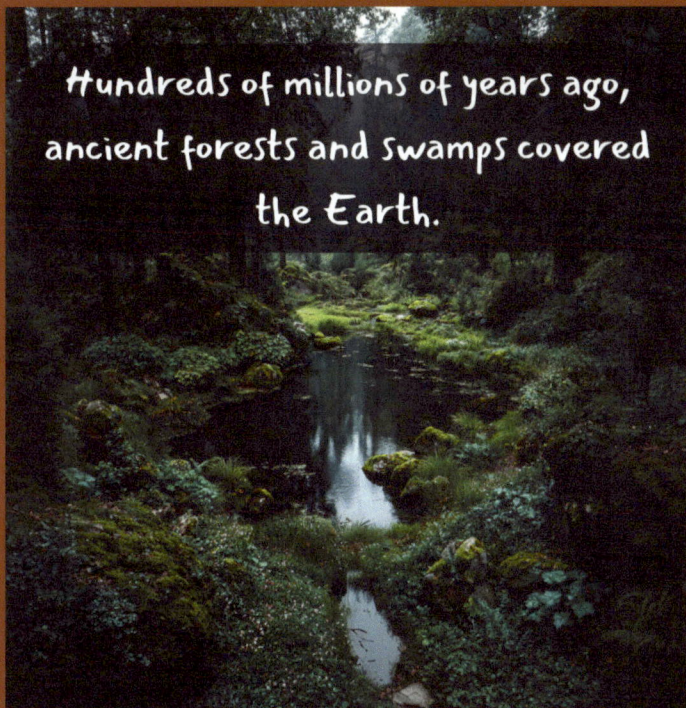

Over time, the plants and trees died.

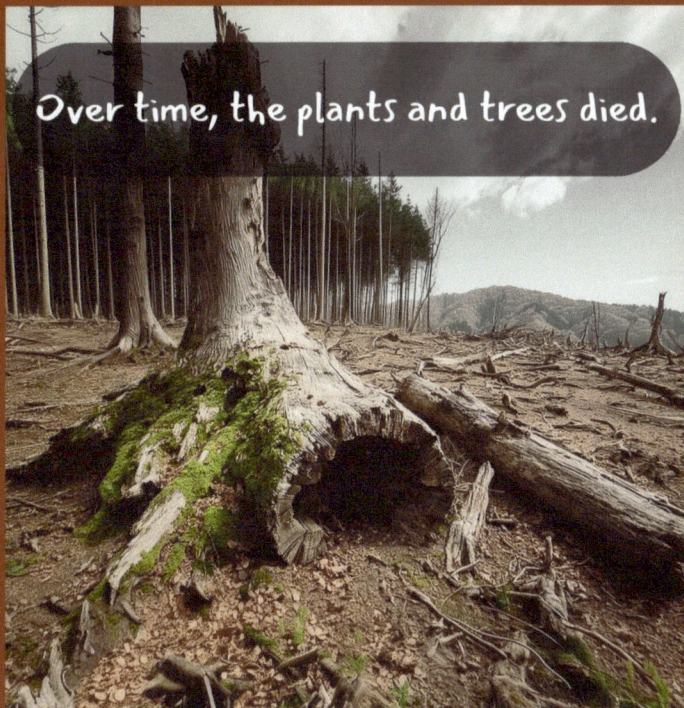

Dead plants, trees, and tiny ocean organisms were buried under layers of mud, sand, and rock.

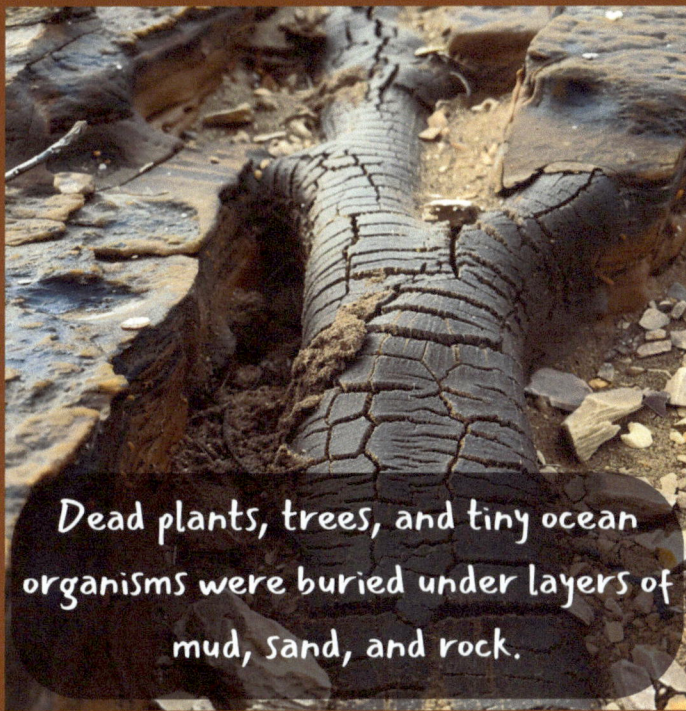

Under intense heat and pressure, the organic remains were changed into fuels like coal, oil, and natural gas.

Fossil Fuel Power Plants

In coal-fired power plants, coal is burned to heat water. Once the water boils, it creates steam that spins the blades on a turbine to create energy. This energy is then used to power a generator that creates the electricity.

In natural gas power plants, natural gas is burned to heat water. Similar to coal-fired power plants, once the water boils, it creates steam that spins the blades of a turbine to create energy, which drives a generator to create electricity.

A Coal-fired Power Plant

A Natural Gas-fired Power Plant

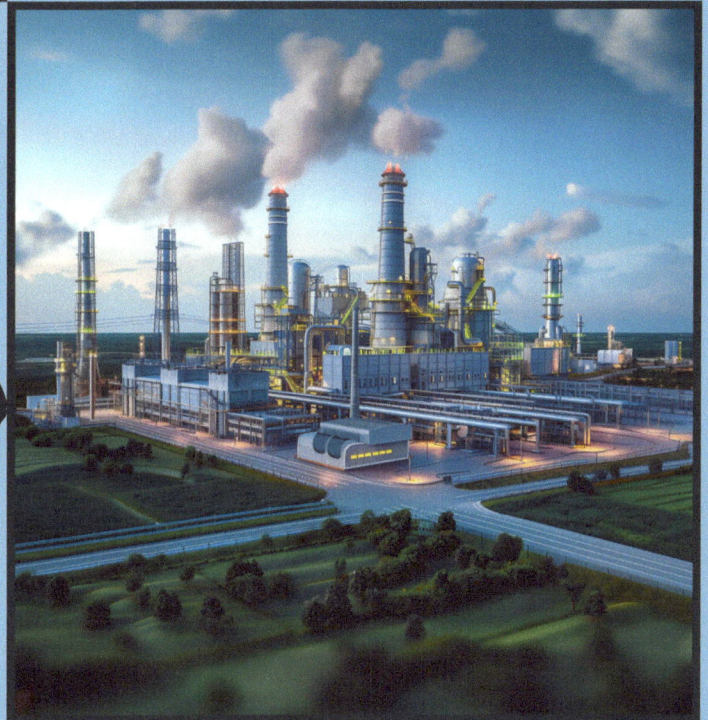

Nuclear Power Plants

In nuclear power plants, a controlled nuclear reaction is used to create heat. This heat is then used to boil water to produce steam. The steam then turns the huge blades of a turbine, which powers a generator to make electricity.

Hydroelectric Power Plants

At hydroelectric power plants, electricity is generated with moving water. Water flowing through a pipe is used to push against and turn the blades of a turbine. The spinning blades power a generator that makes the electricity.

Turbines can also be placed in rivers, where the push from the river's current spins the turbine blades, which then drives a generator to create electricity.

A Nuclear Power Plant

A Hydro-electric Power Plant

Unlike water, which we can store in a tank, electricity cannot be stored in large amounts. This means electricity must be used almost immediately after it is made. When you turn on a light switch, power plants somewhere are creating that exact electricity at that exact moment to power your light bulb.

Renewable Energy.

We get renewable energy from Mother Nature.

It comes from resources that naturally will be replaced again, like the wind and the sun, and then we use this energy to create electricity.

The benefit of using renewable energy is that it will never run out. It's also clean, because it doesn't pollute the air or the water around us.

Let's take a look at the most common sources of renewable energy.

Renewable Energy

<u>Solar Power</u>: By catching the sun's energy with special equipment called solar panels, we can change sunlight directly into electricity.

<u>Wind Power</u>: We use the wind to turn large blades on wind turbines to create energy. This energy is then used to power generators that create electricity.

<u>Geothermal Power</u>: We can also use the heat from the Earth's core to make electricity. At geothermal power stations, heat from below the Earth's surface is used to heat water to create steam. The steam is then used to turn the blades of a turbine, and the energy created by the spinning turbine is used to drive a generator to make electricity.

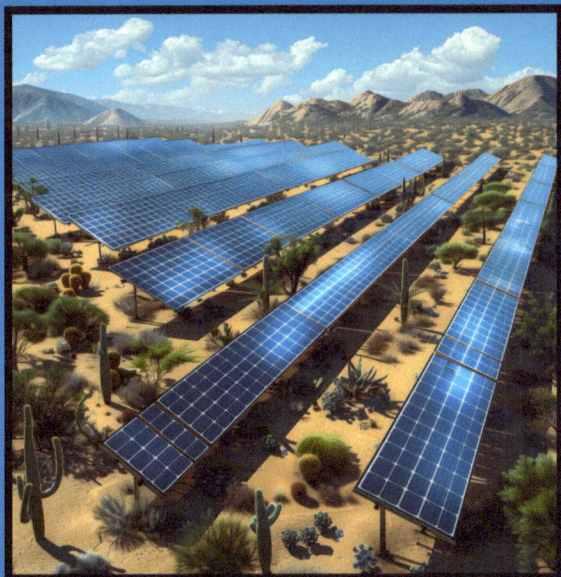

Solar Panels

Wind Turbines

Geothermal Power Generation

In most cases, when electricity is generated, there is a lot of smoke, pollution, and noise created by the power plant.

When we use hydroelectric power plants, they have to be built close to rivers or dams.

That's why, most of the time, power plants are built far away from where we live, and the electricity has to be transported over long distances to our towns and cities.

The electricity travels from power plants to our towns and cities through special cables called transmission lines. Since electricity usually has to travel over long distances to get to the city, it is transported at high voltage, so that more electricity can be transported at the same time.

Voltage is like the pressure that pushes electric current to flow in a wire between two points. Higher voltage creates a stronger push, allowing more electricity to flow through the wire. Lower voltage creates a weaker push, resulting in less electricity flowing through the wire.

Think of it like water flowing through a garden hose. High voltage is like high water pressure that pushes more water through the pipe, while lower voltage is like low water pressure that pushes less water through the pipe.

High-voltage transmission lines are almost like highways for electricity, and they can be constructed above ground by using tall towers to support the electric cables, or underground, by burying the electric cables.

Although power plants generate electricity at high voltage to make sure it can travel fast over long distances, high voltage electricity is very unsafe, and most of our appliances won't work well with it.

For this reason, high voltage electricity has to be changed to low voltage electricity before we can use it in our homes and businesses. Once the transmission lines reach the town or city, they carry the electricity to substations.

Substations are buildings that hold special equipment called transformers. Transformers are clever devices that change the electricity from high voltage to low voltage.

Once the voltage is changed, it is safe to distribute the electricity all over town.

An Electrical Substation

A Voltage Transformer

Distribution lines are the last step of electricity's journey, carrying the electricity from the substations directly to our neighborhoods, businesses, and homes.

Unlike the high voltage transmission lines, distribution lines operate at much lower voltages, making sure it's safe for people and equipment, while still providing enough electricity to power our homes.

Distribution lines can also be constructed either overhead or underground, and they may also include smaller transformers that further reduce the voltage. These transformers are usually mounted on poles or concrete pads in our neighborhoods.

Suburban Electric Distribution Lines

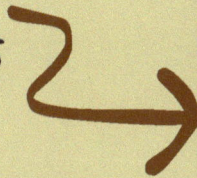

A Pad-mounted Electrical Transformer

Now you know how electricity is made and how it is transported to our homes. Next time you turn on the television or your game console, try to imagine the journey electricity had to take to get to your house so you could play your favorite games!

It's always very important to remember that electricity can be very dangerous to work with.

You should never touch electrical outlets or damaged wires, never play with water close to electricity, and always ask an adult for help with electrical appliances.

Careers in Power Generation

If you care about powering our communities reliably while protecting the environment through clean energy, then careers dedicated to power generation might be perfect for you! There are many exciting jobs for people who want to help create the systems that turn natural resources like sunlight, wind, and water into the electricity that powers our homes, schools, and businesses. Here are examples of careers that work together to generate every bit of electricity we need while keeping our air and water clean for future generations.

Engineering & Design:

- Electrical Engineer - Designs electrical systems for power plants and transmission networks. Creates blueprints for generators, transformers, and power distribution systems.

- Power Systems Engineer - Plans and designs entire electrical grids. Figure out how to connect power plants to cities and make sure electricity flows reliably to everyone.

- Mechanical Engineer - Designs and builds the moving parts of power plants, like turbines, pumps, and cooling systems. Works on making machines run efficiently and safely.

- Civil Engineer - Builds the structures that house power plants, including dams for hydroelectric plants, foundations for wind turbines, and buildings for nuclear facilities.

- Nuclear Engineer - Specializes in designing nuclear reactors and ensuring they operate safely. Plans how nuclear fuel will be used and stored.

- <u>Environmental Engineer</u> - Works to minimize the environmental impact of power generation. Design systems to reduce pollution and protect air and water quality.

- <u>Renewable Energy Engineer</u> - Focuses specifically on solar, wind, and other clean energy technologies. Designs solar panel arrays and wind farms.

<u>Operations & Maintenance:</u>

- <u>Power Plant Operator</u> - Controls the day-to-day operation of power plants. Monitors equipment, adjusts settings, and ensures electricity is generated safely and efficiently.

- <u>Electrical Technician</u> - Maintains and repairs electrical equipment at power plants and substations. Tests systems and fixes problems when they occur..

- <u>Power Line Worker (Lineworker)</u> - Installs, maintains, and repairs the transmission and distribution lines that carry electricity from power plants to homes and businesses.

- <u>Wind Turbine Technician</u> - Climbs wind turbines to perform maintenance and repairs. Ensures wind turbines operate efficiently to generate clean electricity.

- <u>Substation Technician</u> - Maintains the transformers and other equipment at electrical substations that change voltage levels for safe distribution.

Regulatory and Compliance:

- <u>Electrical Safety Inspector</u> - Ensures that electrical systems meet safety codes and regulations. Inspects power plants and electrical installations to prevent accidents.

- <u>Environmental Compliance Officer</u> - Makes sure power plants follow environmental laws and regulations. Monitors pollution levels and ensures companies meet clean air and water standards.

- <u>Nuclear Regulatory Inspector</u> - Specializes in nuclear power plant safety. Conducts inspections and ensures nuclear facilities follow strict safety protocols.

- <u>Energy Policy Analyst</u> - Studies energy laws and regulations. Helps create policies about how electricity should be generated and distributed fairly and safely.

Research and Development:

- <u>Energy Research Scientist</u> - Develops new ways to generate electricity more efficiently and cleanly. Conducts experiments with new technologies and materials.

- <u>Renewable Energy Researcher</u> - Focuses on improving solar, wind, and other clean energy technologies. Studies ways to make renewable energy more affordable and reliable.

- <u>Environmental Scientist</u> - Studies how power generation affects the environment. Develops solutions to reduce the environmental impact of electricity production.

Power Generation Glossary

A glossary is like a mini-dictionary of terms with definitions.

Here's a glossary of terms associated with Power Generation.

Battery - A device that stores electrical energy and can release it when needed. Like a container that holds electricity for later use.

Circuit - A complete path that electricity follows to flow from one place to another. Like a circle or loop that electricity travels around.

Coal - A black rock formed from ancient plants that burned millions of years ago. When burned, it creates heat to make steam for generating electricity.

Current - The flow of electricity through wires. Think of it like water flowing through a pipe, but instead of water, tiny particles called electrons are moving.

Dam - A wall built across a river to control water flow. Dams create lakes behind them and can be used to generate electricity with water power.

Distribution Lines - The electrical wires that carry electricity from substations to homes, schools, and businesses in neighborhoods. These operate at lower, safer voltages.

Electric Grid - The entire system of power plants, transmission lines, substations, and distribution lines that work together to bring electricity to everyone who needs it.

Electricity - A form of energy created by moving electrons. It powers lights, computers, refrigerators, and almost everything we plug into wall outlets.

Energy - The ability to do work or make things happen. Energy can make things move, heat up, light up, or change in other ways.

Fossil Fuel - Coal, oil, and natural gas formed from ancient plants and sea creatures that died millions of years ago. These fuels can be burned to create electricity.

Generator - A machine that creates electricity by using spinning magnets and coils of wire. When turbines spin the generator, it produces electrical power.

Geothermal Power - Electricity made using heat from deep inside the Earth. Hot rocks underground heat water to create steam that spins turbines.

Hydroelectric Power - Electricity created using moving water. Water flows through turbines to spin generators that make electrical power.

Kilowatt - A unit that measures electrical power. One kilowatt can power about ten 100-watt light bulbs at the same time.

Megawatt - A unit that measures large amounts of electrical power. One megawatt equals 1,000 kilowatts and can power about 1,000 homes.

Natural Gas - A fossil fuel that burns cleanly to create heat. It's used in power plants to boil water and create steam for generating electricity.

Nuclear Power - Electricity created using the energy stored inside atoms. Nuclear reactions create heat that boils water to make steam for spinning turbines.

Pollution - Harmful substances released into the air, water, or ground. Some power plants create pollution, while renewable energy sources create very little.

Power - Another word for electricity. The energy that flows through wires to make lights turn on and machines work.

Power Generation - The process of making or creating electricity. This happens at power plants using various energy sources.

Power Plant - A facility or factory where electricity is generated. Different types of power plants use different energy sources to create electrical power.

Reactor - The part of a nuclear power plant where nuclear reactions happen safely. It's surrounded by thick walls to contain the nuclear process.

Renewable Energy - Energy that comes from natural sources that never run out, like sunlight, wind, and flowing water. These sources can be used over and over again.

Solar Panel - A flat device that captures sunlight and changes it directly into electricity. Many solar panels together can power homes and businesses.

Solar Power - Electricity created by capturing energy from the sun. Solar panels contain special materials that turn sunlight into electrical power.

Steam - Water that has been heated until it becomes a gas. Steam is used to spin turbines in many types of power plants.

Substation - A facility that contains transformers and other equipment to change electricity from high voltage to lower, safer voltages for distribution.

Transformer - A device that changes electricity from one voltage to another. Transformers make high-voltage electricity safe for use in homes and schools.

Transmission Lines - Large electrical wires held up by tall towers that carry electricity over long distances from power plants to cities and towns.

Turbine - A machine with blades that spin when pushed by steam, water, or wind. As turbines spin, they turn generators to create electricity.

Voltage - The force or pressure that pushes electricity through wires. Like water pressure in pipes, higher voltage pushes electricity with more force.

Watt - The basic unit for measuring electrical power. A typical light bulb uses about 60 to 100 watts of electricity.

Wind Power - Electricity created using moving air. Wind pushes against large turbine blades, causing them to spin generators that make electrical power.

Wind Turbine - A tall structure with large blades that spin when the wind blows. As the blades turn, they operate a generator to create electricity.

The Journey of Electricity Quiz

<u>Multiple Choice (Choose the best answer)</u>

1. What are power plants often called?
   a) Energy stores
   b) Electricity factories
   c) Power houses
   d) Generation centers

2. Which fossil fuel is described as a black rock?
   a) Coal
   b) Oil
   c) Natural gas
   d) Steam

3. What spins the blades of a turbine in a coal-fired power plant?
   a) Wind
   b) Steam
   c) Water
   d) Natural gas

4. How do generators create electricity?
   a) By burning coal
   b) By using magnets and coils of wire
   c) By heating water
   d) By storing energy

5. Which energy source will never run out?
   a) Coal
   b) Natural gas
   c) Nuclear fuel
   d) Renewable energy

6. What is voltage similar to?
   a) Water temperature in pipes
   b) Water pressure in pipes
   c) Water volume in pipes
   d) Water color in pipes

7. Where does electricity get changed from high voltage to low voltage?
   a) Power plants
   b) Distribution lines
   c) Substations
   d) Transmission lines

8. What do transformers do?
   a) Generate electricity
   b) Store electricity
   c) Change voltage levels
   d) Transport electricity

9. Unlike water, electricity cannot be:
   a) Generated
   b) Transported
   c) Used safely
   d) Stored in large amounts

10. Which type of power uses heat from deep underground?
   a) Solar power
   b) Wind power
   c) Geothermal power
   d) Hydroelectric power

11. What do solar panels capture to make electricity?
   a) Wind
   b) Sunlight
   c) Water
   d) Steam

12. Who designs the moving parts of power plants?
   a) Electrical engineers
   b) Mechanical engineers
   c) Civil engineers
   d) Nuclear engineers

13. Which job involves climbing wind turbines?
   a) Power plant operator
   b) Electrical technician
   c) Wind turbine technician
   d) Substation technician

14. Who ensures power plants follow environmental laws?
   a) Environmental compliance officer
   b) Energy policy analyst
   c) Nuclear regulatory inspector
   d) Electrical safety inspector

15. What measures large amounts of electrical power?
   a) Kilowatt
   b) Watt
   c) Megawatt
   d) Voltage

16. High-voltage transmission lines are like:
   a) Highways for electricity
   b) Storage tanks for electricity
   c) Factories for electricity
   d) Filters for electricity

17. What are fossil fuels mainly formed from?
   a) Dinosaurs only
   b) Ancient plants and tiny sea creatures
   c) Rocks and minerals
   d) Modern plants

18. Nuclear power plants use what type of reaction?
   a) Chemical reaction
   b) Electrical reaction
   c) Nuclear reaction
   d) Steam reaction

19. Distribution lines operate at:
   a) High voltage
   b) Medium voltage
   c) Low voltage
   d) Variable voltage

20. What do hydroelectric power plants use to generate electricity?
   a) Steam
   b) Wind
   c) Sunlight
   d) Moving water

21. Who studies how power generation affects the environment?
   a) Environmental scientist
   b) Energy research scientist
   c) Renewable energy researcher
   d) Power systems engineer

22. Turbines are a type of:
   a) Generator
   b) Engine
   c) Transformer
   d) Circuit

23. What unit measures basic electrical power?
   a) Megawatt
   b) Kilowatt
   c) Watt
   d) Voltage

24. A complete path that electricity follows is called a:
   a) Grid
   b) Circuit
   c) Current
   d) Generator

25. Who installs and repairs transmission lines?
   a) Electrical technician
   b) Power plant operator
   c) Power line worker
   d) Substation technician

26. A _____ is a machine that creates electricity by using spinning magnets and coils of wire.

27. _____ power uses moving water to generate electricity.

28. Coal is formed from _____ plants that died millions of years ago.

29. A _____ is a device that changes electricity from one voltage to another.

30. _____ energy comes from natural sources that never run out.

31. Solar panels capture _____ and change it directly into electricity.

32. The force that pushes electricity through wires is called _____.

33. _____ lines carry electricity over long distances from power plants to cities.

34. A _____ is a wall built across a river to control water flow.

35. _____ is water that has been heated until it becomes a gas.

36. Wind _____ have large blades that spin when the wind blows.

37. A _____ measures electrical power and equals 1,000 watts.

38. The entire system that brings electricity to everyone is called the electric _____.

39. _____ power plants use controlled nuclear reactions to create heat.

40. A _____ is a complete path that electricity follows to flow from one place to another.

41. _____ gas is a fossil fuel that burns cleanly to create heat.

42. Electrical _____ maintain and repair electrical equipment at power plants.

43. _____ power uses heat from deep inside the Earth.

44. A power plant _____ controls the day-to-day operation of power plants.

45. _____ lines carry electricity from substations directly to homes and businesses.

46. The part of a nuclear power plant where reactions happen safely is called the _____.

47. A _____ can power about 1,000 homes.

48. _____ fuel power plants burn coal or natural gas to generate electricity.

49. Moving _____ flows through wires when electricity travels from one place to another.

50. Environmental _____ officers make sure power plants follow environmental laws.

True/False (Write T for True or F for False)

51. Electricity can be stored in large amounts like water in a tank. _____

52. Renewable energy sources create very little pollution. _____

53. High voltage electricity is safe to use in homes. _____

54. When you turn on a light switch, electricity must be created at that exact moment. _____

55. All power plants create smoke, pollution, and noise. _____

56. Fossil fuels are formed mainly from dinosaurs. _____

57. Wind turbine technicians climb wind turbines to perform maintenance. _____

58. Transformers are only found at power plants. _____

59. Solar panels work by using magnets and coils of wire. _____

60. Hydroelectric power plants must be built close to rivers or dams. _____

61. One megawatt equals 100 kilowatts. _____

62. Distribution lines operate at lower voltages than transmission lines. _____

63. Geothermal power uses heat from the sun. _____

64. Nuclear engineers design nuclear reactors. _____

65. Voltage is similar to water pressure in pipes. _____

66. Power line workers install and maintain transmission lines. _____

67. Coal is described as a white rock. _____

68. Energy is the ability to do work. _____

69. Electrical safety inspectors ensure power plants meet safety codes. _____

70. Turbines use moving fluids to spin blades. _____

Quiz Answer Key

Multiple Choice	Fill-in-the-Blank	True/False
1. b	26. generator	51. False
2. a	27. Hydroelectric	52. True
3. b	28. ancient	53. False
4. b	29. transformer	54. True
5. d	30. Renewable	55. False
6. b	31. sunlight	56. False
7. c	32. voltage	57. True
8. c	33. Transmission	58. False
9. d	34. dam	59. False
10. c	35. Steam	60. True
11. b	36. turbines	61. False
12. b	37. kilowatt	62. True
13. c	38. grid	63. False
14. a	39. Nuclear	64. True
15. c	40. circuit	65. True
16. a	41. Natural	66. True
17. b	42. technicians	67. False
18. c	43. Geothermal	68. True
19. c	44. operator	69. True
20. d	45. Distribution	70. True
21. a	46. reactor	
22. b	47. megawatt	
23. c	48. Fossil	
24. b	49. current	
25. c	50. compliance	

Take a look at other subjects Lila and Andy are learning about...

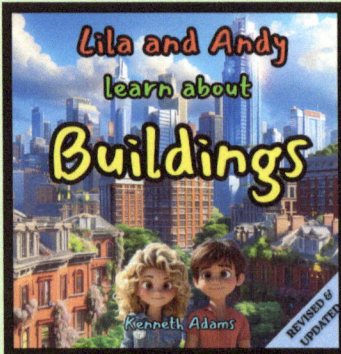
Lila and Andy learn about Buildings — Kenneth Adams (REVISED & UPDATED)

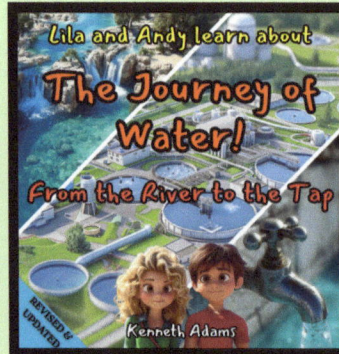
Lila and Andy learn about The Journey of Water! From the River to the Tap — Kenneth Adams (REVISED & UPDATED)

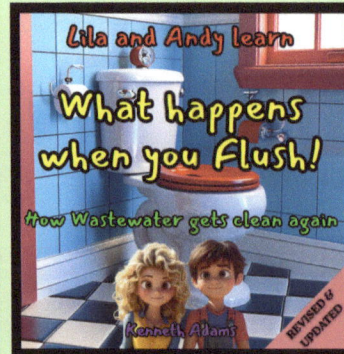
Lila and Andy learn What happens when you Flush! How Wastewater gets clean again — Kenneth Adams (REVISED & UPDATED)

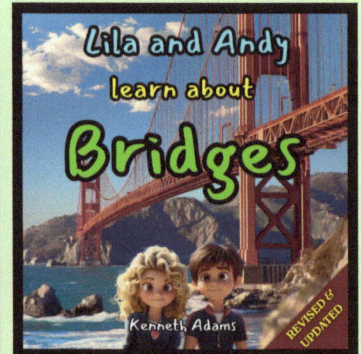
Lila and Andy learn about Bridges — Kenneth Adams (REVISED & UPDATED)

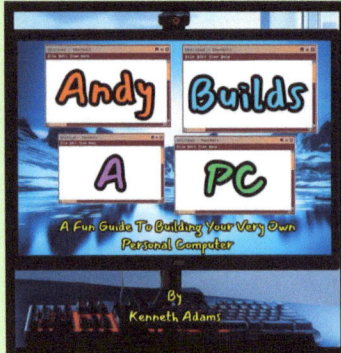
Andy Builds A PC — A Fun Guide To Building Your Very Own Personal Computer — By Kenneth Adams

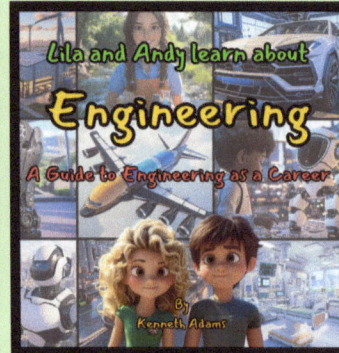
Lila and Andy learn about Engineering — A Guide to Engineering as a Career — By Kenneth Adams

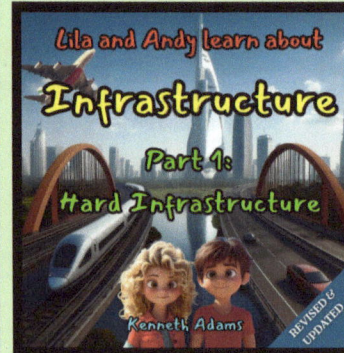
Lila and Andy learn about Infrastructure Part 1: Hard Infrastructure — Kenneth Adams (REVISED & UPDATED)

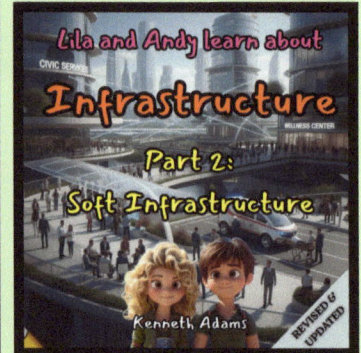
Lila and Andy learn about Infrastructure Part 2: Soft Infrastructure — Kenneth Adams (REVISED & UPDATED)

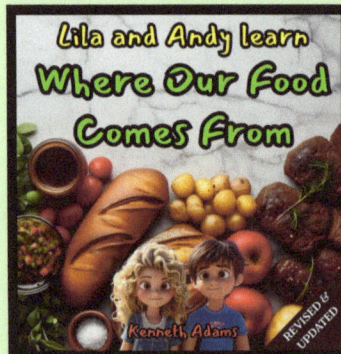
Lila and Andy learn Where Our Food Comes From — Kenneth Adams (REVISED & UPDATED)

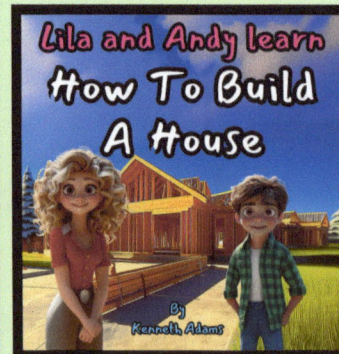
Lila and Andy learn How To Build A House — By Kenneth Adams

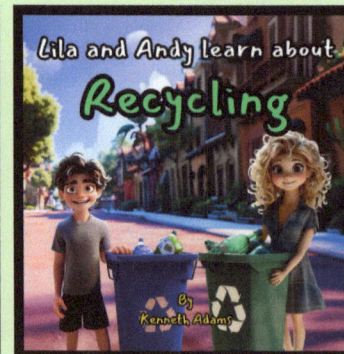
Lila and Andy learn about Recycling — By Kenneth Adams

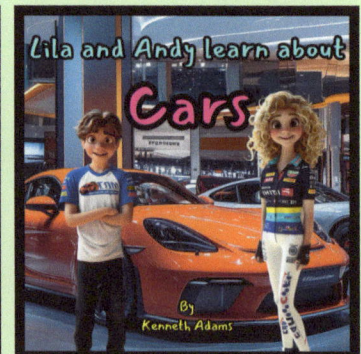
Lila and Andy learn about Cars — By Kenneth Adams

Lila and Andy learn about
Safety on Ice
By Kenneth Adams

Lila and Andy learn about
Winter Roads
By Kenneth Adams

Lila and Andy learn about
Smart Cities
By Kenneth Adams

Lila and Andy learn about
Digital Networks
How the Internet Connects Us
By Kenneth Adams

Lila and Andy learn about
Biomimicry
Kenneth Adams

Lila and Andy learn about
Artificial Intelligence
Discover Large Language Models and Prompt Engineering
By Kenneth Adams

Lila and Andy learn about
Climate Change
Understand Our Changing Planet
Kenneth Adams

Lila and Andy learn about
Environmental Science
Protecting Earth Through Science
Kenneth Adams

Lila and Andy learn about
The Carbon Cycle
Kenneth Adams

Lila and Andy learn about
Data Science & Cryptography
Kenneth Adams

Lila and Andy Present
Fun And Challenging Activities For Kids
An Awesome STEM Coloring and Puzzle Book for Aspiring Engineers and Scientists
Kenneth Adams

THE DEFINITIVE
STEM CHALLENGE WORKBOOK
FOR ADULTS AND TEENS
An Exciting Mix of Mind-Stimulating STEM Challenges for All Skill Levels.
Crosswords, Word Searches, Sudoku, Mazes, and Much More to Sharpen Your Mind and Train Your Brain!
Kenneth Adams

THE DEFINITIVE
TRAVEL ACTIVITY BOOK
GEOGRAPHY PUZZLES FOR ALL AGES
An Exciting Mix of Mind-Stimulating Geography Challenges for All Skill Levels.
Map Challenges, Coloring Pages, Crosswords, Word Searches, and Much More to Make Travel More Enjoyable!
Kenneth Adams

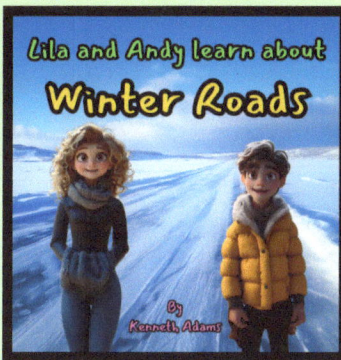

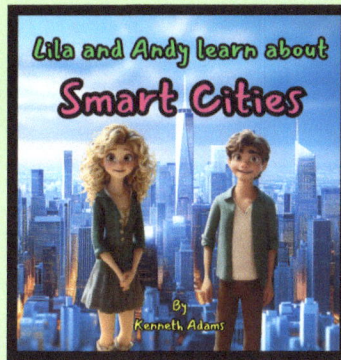

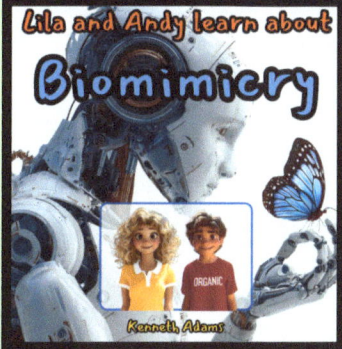

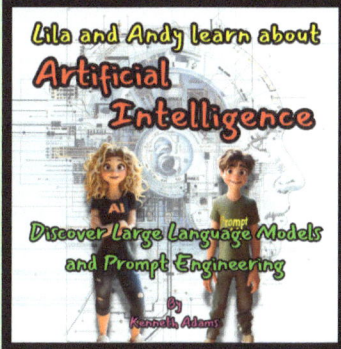

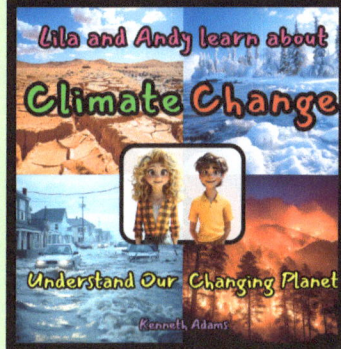

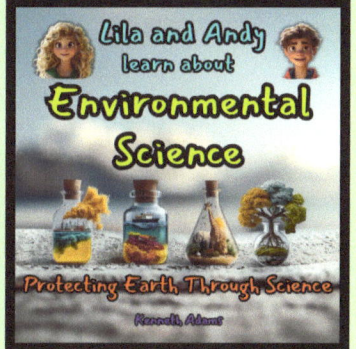

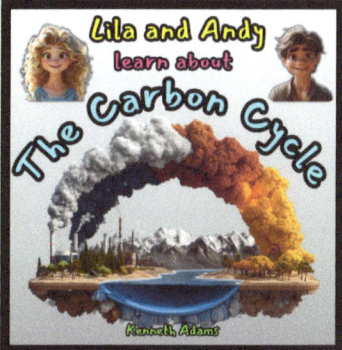

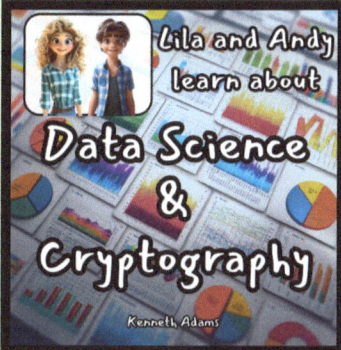

Available on Amazon.

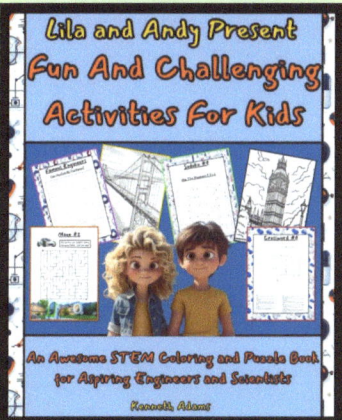

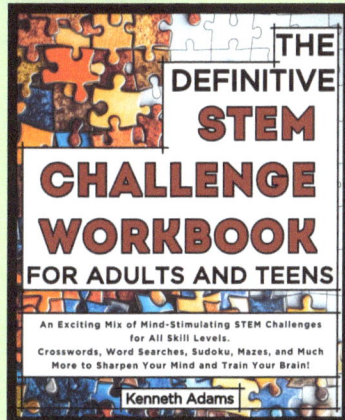

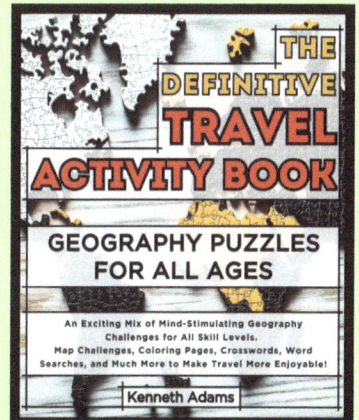

www.ingramcontent.com/pod-product-compliance
Lightning Source LLC
Chambersburg PA
CBHW040916100426
42737CB00042B/94